Remote & Effective

Sharpening Your Communication in a Digital World

Table of Contents

Chapter 1. Introduction

Discover the art of effective communication in today's digital era with our Special Report - "Remote & Effective: Sharpening Your Communication in a Digital World". As the landscape of our conversations shifts onto screens and keyboards, maintaining clarity, creating impact, and fostering meaningful interactions now come with a whole new playbook. This report unveils the techniques to overcome these challenges, imbuing your communications with effectiveness and human touch, even when conveyed through digital platforms. Packed with research, practical guidance, expert insights, and actionable strategies, this is an indispensable guide whether you're a digital novice or a seasoned remote professional. Add fluency to your digital language and let your communication create ripples in the virtual world!

Chapter 2. Mastering the Basics of Digital Communication

In this age of rapid technological advancements, our interactions have been ushered into a realm comprised largely of screens and keyboards. Traditional modes of communication have been significantly surpassed by digital forms, requiring individuals to add a crucial arrow to their quiver - digital fluency. In essence, mastering the basics of digital communication is not a choice but a necessity. Here's how you can accomplish that.

2.1. Understanding the Digital Language

Before we dive into strategies, it's crucial to understand what constitutes digital language. Unlike in face-to-face conversations where our words are supplemented with vocal intonation, body language, and even facial expressions, in digital communication, your words are your only weapon and shield. A clear understanding of the nuances of the digital language will empower you to communicate effectively to achieve your objectives.

Write succinctly yet clearly, preferring simple words to jargon, short sentences to long ones, and always be conscious of your tone – even if it might not seem as important in text, your choice of words can imply a tone that might be perceived differently.

2.2. Embrace the Brevity

In our increasingly connected world, attention spans are dwindling.

Conveying your message concisely is the key to ensuring its consumption. Respect your recipient's time and sharpen your point quickly. Brevity does not mean sacrificing clarity or precision. It's an art of delivering what's needed in the least possible but most effective words.

To master this, understand your objective clearly — what precise action or response do you want your communication to induce? Having your end goal in mind will ensure you devise messages that hit the mark.

2.3. Orchestrating Virtual Meetings

Virtual meetings have become the mainstay of professional communication. Knitting a productive meeting requires careful planning and execution. Set clear objectives, share the agenda in advance, decide on and communicate the platform and timings with clear instructions on how to participate. Stick to the schedule as much as possible during the meeting. Provide time for participants to prepare their thoughts and encourage participation.

Make sure to have a quiet environment to avoid unnecessary distractions. Use reliable internet connectivity to avoid glitches during the meeting. These small measures can significantly enhance the effectiveness of your virtual meetings.

2.4. Navigating Email Etiquettes

Emails are a fundamental part of digital communication, yet the most mishandled. From a catchy subject line that ensures your mail isn't lost in a swarm of unread emails to a concise body that delivers your message effectively, mastering email communication is crucial.

Always begin with a proper salutation before getting into the subject matter. Don't forget to include a simple thank you or a sign-off line at the end of your email. Make sure your email is free from grammatical errors. Also, remember to reply promptly to your emails, maintaining the thread for the sake of continuity.

2.5. Utilizing Social Media Platforms

Social media platforms provide a potent channel for digital communication these days. Whether it's LinkedIn for professional connections, Twitter for short updates, or Instagram for visual content, each platform comes with its language, norms, and best practices.

Know your platforms and tailor your communication to suit the audience on each. Use hashtags effectively. Engage with users, respond to comments, and always maintain a conversational tone. Your authenticity on these platforms can go a long way in ensuring effective communication.

2.6. Decoding the Art of Messaging

Though informal, messaging apps like WhatsApp, Slack, or even direct messages on social media, are progressively being used for professional communication. The art here is to balance the informal tone prevalent on these platforms with professionalism.

Don't use too many abbreviations, as it could lead to confusion. Maintain professionalism in your choice of words and emotions. Also, timely responses are a must, especially during working hours.

The key to mastering digital communication lies in continuous learning and adapting. With every tweet you craft, every email you write, or every virtual meeting you conduct, there's a lesson to be learned. Be open, be mindful, and keep improving!

In the end, remember that while technology provides various

channels each with their own unique rules, the essence of communication doesn't change. Your goal is still to make yourself understood and understand others. The tools of effective communication - clarity, brevity, respect for your recipient's time, active listening - remain the same whether you are meeting face-to-face or sending a tweet.

Chapter 3. Tailoring Messages for Diverse Platforms

Treating each digital platform as a unique entity is an essential aspect of creating effective messages. While there is a certain overlap in the user base of different platforms, each has a unique culture and expectations. The micro-messages that work on Twitter might not have the same effect on LinkedIn, where comprehensive, thought-out content typically performs better. Similarly, Facebook values community engagement and shareable content, while Instagram attracts users with visually appealing content.

3.1. Understanding Different Digital Platforms

Before you can tailor messages for different platforms, an understanding of their unique characteristics is crucial. Let's dive into the peculiarities of some of the common digital platforms.

Twitter is a fast-paced platform dedicated to conversation and ideas. Users often engage with timely, relevant content that can range from serious to fun and conversational.

LinkedIn is a professional network, primarily catering to B2B audiences. Educational, industry-related, and career development content works well here.

Facebook and **Instagram**, both owned by Meta, focus more on personal connections and visual content. While Facebook is community-oriented, Instagram emphasizes aesthetics and lifestyle. Emotive, personalized content can perform well on these platforms.

The varied nature of these platforms indicates the need for a tailored messaging approach for each.

3.2. Tailoring Messages for Twitter

Twitter favors pithy, impactful content. A good tweet captures the essence of your message in a clear, concise, and engaging manner, taking full advantage of the 280-character limit.

Hashtags can help categorize your content, making it discoverable by those interested in similar topics. However, they should be used judiciously as too many can make a post seem cluttered or promotional.

3.3. Tailoring Messages for LinkedIn

LinkedIn messages should be informative, professional, and add value to your audience. It's an ideal platform to share thought leadership content, industry insights, and company news.

Posts should invite engagement, whether it be through questions, invites to comment, or sharing knowledge. As LinkedIn allows for more extensive content compared to Twitter, utilize this to dive deeper into topics and present well-rounded viewpoints.

3.4. Tailoring Messages for Facebook

Unlike LinkedIn, the content on Facebook is more casual and community focused. Your messaging here should foster a sense of community and engage users in a relevant, meaningful way. Facebook's strength is in creating relationships and fostering discussions.

Use various content types like posts, polls, live videos, stories, or infographics, to encourage audience engagement. Remember, on Facebook, every reaction, comment, or share increases your content's visibility.

3.5. Tailoring Messages for Instagram

Instagram is all about the visuals. Even if the actual message is compelling, poor visuals can hamper engagement. Whether it's images, videos or Stories, ensure all visual content is high-quality, with clear messaging.

While Instagram allows for longer captions than Twitter, the first couple of lines matter most – that's what viewers see before deciding to click 'more'. Keep the most critical message upfront and then delve deeper.

3.6. Other Considerations for Tailoring Messages

Apart from platform-specific considerations, other important factors come to play in messaging. These include understanding your target audience, relevance and timing of your message, and how you incite engagement. Practice, trial and error, and feedback will refine your messaging strategies over time.

Creating effective communication in a digital world doesn't mean simply crafting messages. Rather, it involves recognizing the nature of the platform, the intent of its users, and coming up with a strategy that successfully mingles the two. It's about striking a balance between the medium, the message, and the manner.

3.7. Conclusion

In a time when digital platforms are merging the personal and professional, the effective communication of your message across these platforms can be a game-changer. The key lies in understanding the atmosphere of each platform and tailoring your message to suit it. Whether it's a tweet, a LinkedIn article, a Facebook post, or an Instagram story, the right messaging can have a resonating impact on your audience, cementing your position as a poignant voice in the digital sphere.

Chapter 4. Emotional Intelligence in Virtual Communication

In the arena of virtual communication, Emotional Intelligence (EI) stands as a cornerstone upon which successful interactions hinge. Unlike face-to-face interactions, where the subtlety of body language, tone nuances, and instant feedback are available, virtual communication often sacrifices such details, with its customary reliance on written text.

Understanding and honing Emotional Intelligence can help build closer connections, enhance comprehension, mitigate misunderstandings, foster empathy, and improve overall communication quality. In the vast canvas of virtual interactions ranging from emails and messages to video conferences and social media comments, the effective use of emotional intelligence is not a luxury, but a necessity.

4.1. The Nuances of Emotional Intelligence

Emotional Intelligence comprises four key elements: self-awareness, self-management, social awareness, and relationship management. Let's explore each of these in relation to virtual communication.

Self-awareness refers to our capacity to identify our own emotions and their effects on our thoughts and actions. In virtual interactions, it is crucial to be mindful of emotional state, as it can influence how we interpret messages or how we frame our responses. A heightened self-awareness also allows us to pause and evaluate our reactions, permitting more thoughtful responses which can be pivotal in a virtual environment, given the permanent nature of digital interactions.

Self-management, the second component, is about managing our emotions, particularly during stressful scenarios or contentious exchanges. In virtual communications, the anonymity of screens can unfortunately enable us to lash out without thinking about the consequences. Mastery of self-management helps us to maintain calm, rationally process situations and respond in a way that is courteous and composed, maintaining a professional demeanor.

In the context of social awareness, it is about understanding and respecting others' emotions. More challenging in a digital context due to the absence of non-verbal cues, it requires paying heed to subtle hints such as the tone of the language or response time. Responding with empathy and kindness to these cues can be immensely rewarding and relationship affirming.

In terms of relationship management, it involves leveraging our understanding of our own and others' emotions to interact effectively. Knowing when to be patient, when to offer support or when to apologize are all examples of good relationship management.

4.2. Building Emotional Intelligence in Virtual Communication

Now that we are acquainted with the key components of Emotional Intelligence, the next step is to finesse them in the digital landscape. Here's a set of useful, actionable measures you can employ.

In order to enhance self-awareness, practice mindfulness. Be aware of how you're feeling before entering a virtual exchange. Is your mood positive, neutral or negative? How might this affect your interactions? Keeping a log of your emotional states during specific virtual interactions can provide insightful data on patterns that need to be addressed.

Building self-management revolves around the principle of 'Think before you type.' In stressful moments, it's easy to let emotions spill out. Try to shift your attention away from the screen momentarily, take a few deep breaths or step away if you can. Remind yourself the consequences can be extensive, long-lasting and likely to affect real-world relationships too.

In improving social awareness, start with the assumption that everyone is doing their best, especially in challenging circumstances. Their delayed responses or curt messages may be due to reasons beyond your knowledge. Responding with understanding can significantly improve the quality of your interactions.

As for relationship management, thoughtfully craft your messages taking into account the other person's perspective. Regularly check in with your virtual teammates or partners, ask how they're doing, and offer help when appropriate.

4.3. Emotional Intelligence and Body Language

Even though virtual communications usually miss the full range of non-verbal cues, videoconferencing provides a partial solution. While it doesn't wholly replicate face-to-face interactions, the best practices of reading and projecting body language still apply.

When it comes to projecting positive body language, make sure you have good posture and appear relaxed. Maintain eye contact by looking at the camera and use gentle, intentional gestures to underline your points.

In reading body language, pay attention to facial expressions which can reveal a lot about a person's feelings. An uncomfortable shift, averting eye contact, or forceful hand gestures can hint at discomfort or disagreement. Remember, understanding emotions does not necessarily come down to verbal expression, and in these moments your Emotional Intelligence truly comes into play.

4.4. The Intersection of Emotional Intelligence and Cultural Intelligence

In a rapidly globalizing world, our virtual communications are no longer confined by geography. We find ourselves in conversation with individuals from a myriad of cultures, each with their own nuances of communication. Here, a subtle interaction between Emotional Intelligence and Cultural Intelligence (CQ) begins to take place.

Having cultural intelligence means being aware of, understanding, and respecting the different cultural influences that shape people's values, practices, and communication patterns. Your Emotional Intelligence, through self-awareness, self-management, social-awareness and relationship management, can help maneuver the complexities of cultural differences. By insisting on empathy and patience, and avoiding assumptions, EI can complement and augment your CQ, creating more meaningful and respectful cross-cultural communications.

Harnessing the power of Emotional Intelligence in the virtual communication landscape is a journey that requires consistent effort and, inevitably, the navigation through inevitable hiccups along the way. However, the rewards, in terms of more effective, harmonious, and impactful communication, are immeasurable. In this increasingly digital era, Emotional Intelligence does not just enhance communication - it equips you with a global currency for connection, acceptance, and understanding, regardless of physical distance.

Chapter 5. Crafting High-Impact Digital Narratives

The canvas of digital communication has become teeming with opportunities and challenges simultaneously. Expressing our thoughts, ideas, or complex scenarios requires an eloquent command over digital narratives. This entails the ability to grab attention, create engagement, and ensure retention - all from behind a screen.

5.1. Basics of Crafting a Digital Narrative

In the stride of digital revolution, communication no longer revolves around mere words. It's about the story you weave; the narrative you unfold underpinned with compelling illustrations, engaging soundbites, or captivating infographics. This intertwining of story and technology is what shapes a digital narrative. Let's begin by understanding some basic principles of constructing your digital narrative:

1. Compelling Opening: Your opening, often the first few lines, should intrigue your audience enough to continue reading or listening. Ask compelling questions, use gripping anecdotes, or start with a surprising fact.

2. Strategic Story Arc: Consider your narrative as a journey that you're inviting your reader on. Establish a beginning (setup), a middle (conflict or complexity), and an end (resolution).

3. Use of Media: Given the multimedia nature of the digital realm, complement your wordy narrative with engaging images, videos, or emotive soundbites.

4. Immerse and Engage: Encourage interactivity wherever possible. This could include quizzes, polls or even an avenue for open

discussion.

Now, let's dive deeper and learn how to implement these principles effectively.

5.2. Creating a Compelling Opening

Matching the pace of today's digital ecosystem, humans hold an average attention span of just eight seconds. Therefore, crafting an impactful beginning is crucial. Open your narrative with a spark. Share a personal story, a provocative question, or a striking statistic that immediately hooks your audience and persuades them to read on. Balance info-dumping with creating suspense. This will initiate curiosity and incentivize your audience to journey forward with your narrative.

5.3. Building a Strategic Story Arc

A narrative without a structured story arc resembles an aimless ship. Employ an effective sequence - introduce an issue or idea, delve into complications, and finally, present a solution. It's also pivotal to continually raise the stakes. Keep revealing the effects of the conflict, tension, or the problem you've established so the reader feels the necessity to reach the end and find the solution.

5.4. Complementing Narrative with Effective Media

Digital platforms abound with multimedia opportunities - images, videos, podcasts, animated clips, infographics, and more. Be sure to integrate these elements seamlessly into your narrative. Design your media to further illustrate, validate, and support your ideas. Remember not to overwhelm your reader with excessive flashiness; restrained use often has the deepest impact.

5.5. Boosting Audience Engagement

Interactivity empowers your audience to actively engage, be part of your narrative, and build deeper connections. Provide opportunities for interaction whether it's through quizzes, polls, questions, or live chats. Also, ensure your narrative provides value. Teach something new, provide insights, or offer solutions to common problems. Making your readers think or learn can help them feel invested in your narrative.

5.6. Detailed Examples and Case Studies

Tangible examples and case studies can significantly empower your narrative. They provide credibility and allow your audience to envision real-world applications of your ideas. Break down these examples to show how an idea grew, how a solution was applied, or how an issue was resolved.

5.7. Crafting Authentic and Clear Messages

Authenticity in digital communication is a currency of its own. Be honest, transparent, and genuine in your story. Stay consistent in your tone and style. Make sure your words represent you and your values accurately.

Clarity is another pivotal aspect. It's easy for your message to get lost in the abundance of digital noise. Therefore, stay concise and precise. Break complex ideas down into digestible bits.

Learning and mastering the art of crafting high-impact digital narratives may seem daunting at first. However, with practice and patience, you can enhance your ability to transcend the digital noise and let your narratives echo across the digital expanse. Remember, true power lies in your story, the way you weave it and tell it to the world.

Chapter 6. Remote Team Management: A Communication-Centric Approach

In the digital age, managing remote teams effectively goes beyond simply assigning tasks and measuring outcomes. It calls for a renewed focus on communication, a central component that impacts everything from collaborative synergy to individual performance, and from team morale to the overall project success. This chapter delves into the facets of a communication-centric approach to remote team management and explores its critical techniques.

6.1. Understanding the Importance of Effective Communication

Communication forms the backbone of any team, more so in a remote team where face-to-face interactions are sometimes totally absent. It can impact essential aspects of team operations such as clarity of tasks, resolving conflicts, fostering collaboration, and maintaining team morale. In a remote setting, this communication needs to be more frequent, transparent, and multi-dimensional to ensure everyone is on the same page and feels a part of the team. Effective communication also fosters an environment of mutual respect and understanding, crucial for achieving desired objectives.

6.2. Crafting a Communication Strategy

An effective communication strategy is vital for remote team management. It requires planning, consistency, and broad understanding of the medium.

1. Identify Your Tools: Choose the right communication tools to suit your team's needs - synchronous (phone calls, video conferencing) for immediate feedback and discussions, and asynchronous (emails, task management software) for detailed instructions and updates.

2. Define Communication Norms: Establish clear guidelines for communication. This includes response time expectations, the preferred medium for different types of communication, rules for virtual meetings, etc.

3. Regular Check-Ins: Make a routine of regular meetings on a weekly or daily basis, ensuring all team members are updated and heard.

4. Foster Open Communication: Create an environment where employees can freely express their thoughts, ideas, or concerns, which leads to improved problem-solving.

6.3. Enhancing Communication Effectiveness

Once a strategy is in place, the effectiveness of the communication needs to be ensured.

1. Active Listening: This instills a feeling of being understood and valued among team members.

2. Empathy: Demonstrating empathy in communications, especially

in challenging situations, boosts morale.

3. Clear and Concise: Each communication should be clear and to the point, focusing on essentials. This helps reduce misunderstanding and saves time.

4. Constructive Feedback: Make feedback constructive and solution-based to encourage learning and growth.

6.4. Nurturing Collaborative Synergy through Communication

Remote teams often suffer from isolation-induced disconnection. Establishing collaborative synergy engages every member and engenders a sense of camaraderie, essential for productivity and satisfaction.

1. Cross-Team Collaboration: Facilitate interactions between members of different teams. This leads to cross-pollination of ideas, thereby broadening perspectives.

2. Collaborative Tools: Use online platforms that encourage active collaboration, like shared documents, virtual whiteboards, etc.

3. Team-Building Activities: Regularly schedule virtual team activities to encourage bonding.

6.5. Measuring and Improving Communication

Continuous evaluation of communication practices is vital for any remote team. Tools like employee surveys, individual discussions, and feedback sessions help identify scope for improvement.

1. Assess Communication Regularly: Regular assessments can help identify communication gaps and issues early.

2. Feedback: Encourage your team to give feedback on the communication practices. This keeps the process democratic and ensures everyone's needs are taken into account.

3. Monitor the Effect: Pay attention to the outcomes of your strategies. Are there fewer misunderstandings? Improved collaboration? Find out to amend the course if needed.

In the vast digital landscape of the remote work environment, robust and effective communication practices can bridge gaps, fostering a conducive and harmonious space for each team member to excel and grow. Through a communication-centric approach, remote teams can thrive, further cultivating a fruitful remote culture conducive to success in the long run.

Chapter 7. Unraveling the Etiquettes of Online Interaction

The digital era has opened doors to a new mode of communication that has transformed our interactions. With this transformation comes a change in etiquette. To navigate the digital world effectively, it's crucial to understand and put into practice the etiquettes of online interaction.

7.1. Understanding Online Etiquettes

Online etiquettes, also known as netiquettes, refer to the conventions and norms of communication in the digital realm. These etiquettes are crucial in upholding respect and courtesy in all digital interactions, whether they are personal or professional.

Netiquettes are not etched in stone, considering the quick evolution of the digital platform. However, some fundamental aspects revolve around the core principles of universal communication like respect, clarity, and understanding.

7.2. The Importance of Respectful Engagement

Interactions in the digital realm are not inherently different from that in real-life exchanges. Respect stands to be a pillar that upholds effective communication in both settings. Here's how to instill respect in online interactions:

- Use polite language: The tone of online communication is open to interpretation. Without the nuances of body language and tone, text can come off as cold or abrasive. Emphasize courtesy and politeness in your text to avoid misunderstandings.

- Behave professionally: Maintain the same level of professionalism online as you would offline. This applies to communication in emails, social media platforms, and meetings in virtual conference rooms.

- Respect privacy: Just like you wouldn't want someone prying into your personal life, others too value their private space. It's essential to respect the boundaries of privacy in digital communication.

7.3. Achieving Clarity in Online Communication

In the digital world, clarity is king. Misinterpretation is a risk that comes with online interaction, increasing the need for clear and concise communication. Analyze the following areas for enhancing clarity:

- Precise Language: Be as precise as possible to avoid confusion. Abstract or vague words can lead to misunderstandings, hindering the flow of communication.

- Maintain Brevity: Being brief and to the point can drastically improve the quality of your interaction, particularly in the professional setting where time is of great value.

- Use of Visual Aids: When an explanation is complex, using visual aids, like graphs, charts, or infographics, can help facilitate understanding.

7.4. Fostering Mutual Understanding

Mutual understanding is the cornerstone of effective communication. To foster understanding in the digital realm, consider these elements:

- Active Listening: Even in the virtual world, listening is an imperative part of communication. Pay attention to what is being communicated and provide constructive responses.

- Ask for Clarification: If a message is confusing or ambiguous, don't hesitate to ask for clarification. This openness can foster healthy interaction and ensure that your conversations are fruitful and meaningful.

- Promote Open Dialogue: Encouraging open dialogue helps in solving conflicts, building trust, and promoting better understanding.

7.5. Navigating the Terrain of Social Media Etiquettes

Social media is a powerful tool for online interaction, but it requires careful navigation. A few essential etiquettes to remember here include:

- Privacy Settings: Keep tabs on your privacy settings and understand the level of visibility you allow others into your posts.

- Public vs. Private: Understand the difference between public posts or comments and private messaging.

- Posting Considerately: Post updates, comments, photos, or videos that respect and consider the values and opinions of your audience.

Mastering these etiquettes of online interaction can enhance your digital communications significantly. In today's world, where more of our conversations happen online than off, these rules of respect, clarity, and understanding can guide us in maintaining impactful and civil digital interactions.

Chapter 8. Effective Video Conferencing: More than Just Talking

Video conferencing blossomed as one of the principal avenues of communication in the existing digital age. Irrespective of geographical boundaries, it emphasized human connection, eradicating the distance factor. But establishing effective video conferencing demands comprehension that goes beyond the technological aspects and syllables. It's not just about speaking; it's about conveying with efficacy and transforming the experience into a productive meeting that leaves an impact.

8.1. Comprehending the Platform

The underpinning of achieving an influential video conference is comprehending the platform. Familiarizing oneself with the plethora of digital tools available in the market, their features, limitations, and matching them with your needs is the very first step to maximize communication. For instance, while Zoom offers features like breakout rooms, hand-raising, and screen sharing, Google Meet could meet your need if you are looking for a seamless integration with Google Suite.

This decision matrix helps you to compare the different tools on objective parameters.

Tool	Strengths	Weaknesses
Zoom	High quality video and audio, multiple integrations, easy recording.	Ease of hacking, complicated settings.

Tool	Strengths	Weaknesses
Google Meet	Integration with Google Suite, easy to initiate.	Limited features.
Microsoft Teams	Easy scheduling in Outlook, transcription services.	Limited third-party integrations.

Once the platform selection is done, understanding the interface inside out will help you avoid technical glitches on the day of the meeting that may sabotage your intended message.

8.2. Lighting and Presentation

As they say, first impressions are lasting impressions. As much as lighting plays a key role in cinematography, correct lighting is crucial while on a video call to attain that crisp and professional presence. Natural light from the front is the ideal setting but webcams do an excellent job even under low light conditions.

Your surroundings matter as well. A clutter-free background relays a sense of professionalism and discipline. Remember, less is more. Keep distracting items out from view. If there is no choice, make use of the 'blur background' feature available on most platforms.

Think of your physical presentation as viewing yourself from another's perspective. Dress as you would for an in-person meeting. Maintaining eye contact, or towards your camera in this case, is also essential for a genuine connection. Yes, your own video feed is tempting but that distracts from the "eye contact" and can appear disengaged.

8.3. Sound Matters

Strive for crystal clear sound as it is an essential part of your overall communication. A noise-free environment, high-quality microphone, headphones to prevent echo, are some ways to ensure you're heard clearly. Another sound management strategy is to stay on mute when not talking to avoid unwanted noise interrupting the flow of conversation.

8.4. Etiquette and Setting the Tone

Even in a digital setting, ground rules need to be set and followed. Some cultures may require addressing by title. Being mindful of time zones for international attendees and a proper introduction at the onset can set the tone for a fruitful meeting.

8.5. The Power of Body Language

Body language is a subtle yet powerful tool in communication, applicable in digital spaces as well. Earn trust by nodding in this space. Mimic the actions of physically being there - lean in to show involvement, use hands to stress on points, maintaining posture.

8.6. Meaningful Collaboration

Allowing everyone to contribute makes the session interactive and sparks new ideas. Breakout rooms in Zoom or the whiteboard feature in Microsoft Teams can make brainstorming sessions enormously productive. Collaboration tools like Google docs can also be combined for synchronous work.

8.7. Closing the Loop

It's imperative to leave every meeting with clear action items. A brief recap before closure ensures that everyone is on the same page and there are no ambiguities. Sharing minutes of the meeting aids in keeping track of these action items and fosters accountability.

In this ever-evolving landscape of digital communication, effectiveness lies in adapting and incorporating these guidelines. Do not engage in digital communication merely as a necessity but rather as an opportunity to connect, influence, and imprint your ideas on the virtual world.

Remember, every video conference is more than just talking - it's an art of communicating with potency in the digital realm. And as you paint this canvas of digital interaction, these tools are your palette of colors. Paint away, create and connect. Engage in every conversation with preparation and presence, leaving no space for distortion in your digital symphony. Video conferencing is a means to an end - the end is your communication, ringing loud, clear, and equivalently human.

Chapter 9. Digital Communications - Pushing Overall Productivity

In today's world, digital communication has become an integral part of our professional as well as personal lives. When harnessed effectively, it can act as a catalyst to propel overall productivity by leaps and bounds. This chapter will delve into the intricate relationship between digital communication and productivity, elucidating strategies and practices that can enhance individual and organizational output.

9.1. The Intersection of Digital Communication and Productivity

The digital age has transformed the way we communicate and work. The shift from traditional face-to-face interactions to digital dialogues has created a new set of rules for effective communication. However, this transition is not without its challenges.

The efficacy of digital communication lies in its ability to boost productivity. The rapid exchange of information means that team members can make quicker decisions, reduce waiting periods, and optimise workflow. However, it can also lead to information overload and miscommunication if not managed properly.

One must understand that effective digital communication goes beyond sending a clear and concise email—it's about enhancing interactions, fostering understanding, and driving productivity.

9.2. Techniques to Enhance Productivity through Digital Communication

To leverage the full potential of digital communication in boosting productivity, we should effectively employ various strategies and tools at our disposal.

1. Prioritize and Optimize Emails: Emails are a commonly used digital communication medium. Optimizing email communication can have a significant impact on productivity. Avoid sending unnecessary emails and ensure that your messages are clear, concise, and actionable.

2. Utilize Collaboration Tools: Tools like Slack, Microsoft Teams, and Asana enable real-time communication and collaboration. Using these tools enhances transparency and streamlines workflows, increasing overall productivity.

3. Set Clear Communication Guidelines: Establishing clear guidelines about when and how to use different communication platforms reduces confusion and ensures that everyone is on the same page.

4. Maintaining Virtual Etiquettes: Muting microphones when not speaking during virtual meetings, timely response to messages, and keeping discussions relevant can drastically improve the efficiency of digital dialogues.

9.3. Crafting a Productive Digital Communication Culture

The success of digital communication also hinges on the culture within an organization. Creating a culture that encourages open dialogues, respects differences, and supports collaboration can mitigate the risks associated with digital communication, namely isolation and miscommunication.

Here are four actionable steps to foster a digitally productive culture:

1. Encourage Regular Feedback: Regular feedback can improve communication, build trust, and foster a sense of community.

2. Promote Flexibility: With digital platforms offering endless possibilities, allow employees the flexibility to choose the mode of communication suited to their task and personal style.

3. Foster an Inclusive Environment: Ensure everyone can contribute, regardless of their location. Reassuring remote employees that their voices are heard can improve engagement and productivity.

4. Provide Training in Digital Communication: Train team members to communicate effectively on digital platforms, covering areas such as crafting effective emails, conducting productive virtual meetings and understanding digital etiquette.

9.4. The Role of Leadership in Strengthening Digital Communication

The onus of creating a productive digital communication environment also falls on leaders. Strong leadership can foster an environment conducive to productivity by setting good practices in digital communication.

Leaders can promote productivity by:

1. Leading by Example: By showcasing good practices in digital communication, they can set a precedent for the rest of the team.

2. Providing Clarity: By clearly conveying their expectations for

communication, leaders can help prevent misunderstandings that can lead to productivity losses.

3. Fostering Team Cohesion: Leaders can promote team building through shared digital experiences to build rapport and improve collaboration.

4. Prioritizing Mental Health: Recognizing and addressing the risks of digital communication to mental health, such as burnout from excess screen time, leaders can maintain a healthy, and thus more productive, team.

When all the pieces come together—effective techniques, a positive culture, and influential leadership-digital communication can indeed push overall productivity. It becomes a powerful tool in our professional arsenal, enabling us to achieve more with less, making our efforts more fruitful and our work more rewarding.

Digital communication, when executed well, can overcome geographical barriers, streamline workflows and improve productivity. It comes with its own set of challenges, but with the right mindset, guidelines, and tools we can turn these challenges into opportunities to revolutionize the way we work.

Chapter 10. Cultural Sensitivity in Virtual Spaces: A Must-Have Skill

In the digital age, our global connectivity has given rise to incredible advancement and exchange of ideas, crossing geographic boundaries with the click of a button. As such, it becomes infinitely more critical to be sensitive towards an array of diverse cultures as we navigate through our virtual spaces. Cultural sensitivity stands as a vital skill for effective, respectful, and productive communication on these platforms.

10.1. Understanding the Importance of Cultural Sensitivity

A foundation in cultural sensitivity allows us to build bridges in digital spaces, creating an understanding where ignorance and misunderstanding might otherwise exist. It ensures that our messages are interpreted as we intend, and that we understand the messages of those from different cultural backgrounds correctly. In virtual spaces, where non-verbal cues are often missing, culturally sensitive communication is key to avoiding misinterpretations and fostering positive interactions.

This leads to an inclusive environment where every individual feels valued, heard, and seen. This sense of inclusion, in turn, fuels productivity, creativity, and overall job satisfaction. Moreover, it helps to create a more comprehensive perspective by embracing diverse points of view, thereby driving innovation.

10.2. Building Cultural Awareness: The First Step

The first step in learning to be culturally sensitive involves building an awareness of other cultures' norms, practices, and communication styles. It includes understanding that your way isn't the only way, nor is it necessarily the best way. It's this willingness to learn and adapt that will help you interact effectively in a global digital landscape.

Understanding cultural nuances could include anything from knowing business etiquettes in a given culture to acknowledging differing perspectives on time, personal space, or hierarchical structures. Remember, it's not about knowing all; it's about appreciating that differences exist and being open to learning.

10.3. The Role of Active Listening

Active listening is an essential element of cultural sensitivity. It involves paying full attention to the speaker, understanding their message, absorbing it, and responding thoughtfully. Active listening signals respect for the speaker's viewpoint and values, which are vital in fostering cultural sensitivity.

In a virtual space, active listening may involve re-reading messages or emails for comprehension or asking follow-up questions to ensure understanding. The use of feedback and paraphrasing can establish that you have understood the message correctly. Moreover, showing patience and providing space for people to articulate their thoughts can be particularly beneficial when language barriers exist.

10.4. Navigating Language Barriers

Language can often pose a barrier in virtual communication,

especially across cultures. English, while widely spoken, may not be the first language for many participants. The use of jargon or complex language can lead to information loss, misunderstandings, or feelings of exclusion.

To foster inclusivity, try to use simple, clear language in your communication. Encourage others to ask for clarifications if something isn't understood, and similarly, don't hesitate to ask for explanations yourself. The goal is to ensure the message is clear, understood and that everyone feels comfortable in the conversation.

10.5. The Etiquette of Digital Communication Across Cultures

Just as we have social norms in physical spaces, there are norms in digital spaces as well. These norms may vary widely from one culture to another. Understanding and respecting these differences is a crucial aspect of being culturally sensitive.

For example, in some cultures, it may be customary to exchange greetings before diving into the business at hand, while in others, getting straight to the point could be the norm. Similarly, the use of emojis or casual language could be perfectly acceptable in one culture, but considered unprofessional in another.

10.6. Avoiding Assumptions and Stereotypes

Cultural sensitivity involves understanding that not everyone within a culture will believe, behave, or communicate the same way. Stereotypes and assumptions can lead to misunderstanding and may even cause offense.

Instead of basing your interactions on assumptions, approach each conversation with an open mind and ask thoughtful questions. Remember, it's better to ask and clarify than to assume and misconstrue.

10.7. Constantly Learning and Adapting

Cultural sensitivity isn't a one-time endeavor. It requires continuous learning, understanding, questioning and adapting oneself to accommodate differing cultural perspectives. The goal isn't to perfect but to progress consistently, cultivating empathy and respect for all cultures in our increasingly interconnected, digitized world.

In conclusion, cultural sensitivity plays an instrumental role in bridging gaps in understanding and fostering a collaborative, inclusive environment in virtual spaces. It takes conscious effort and commitment to learn, understand, and navigate the intricacies of differing cultural norms but the rewards - successful, compassionate, and inclusive communication - are well worth it. With cultural sensitivity, you're not just talking, you're truly communicating – fostering meaningful and positive intercultural interactions in the digital world.

Chapter 11. Straitening Miscommunications & Building Trust Remotely

In an increasingly digital world, effective communication is a crucial key in reducing misunderstandings and fostering trust, especially in remote processes. Despite the convenience and efficiency that digital platforms bring, they also come with their unique set of challenges.

The first step towards reducing miscommunications is understanding the common scenarios where things tend to go wrong, and learning how to navigate through them. This section presents you with a few such situations and offers solutions to ensure smoother transactions.

11.1. Overcoming Barriers to Communication

Barriers to communication could stem from multiple sources - differing modes of communication, lack of non-verbal communication cues, or technical disruptions. Recognizing and overcoming these barriers is essential to ensure clear, accurate, and impactful communication.

In remote communication, as you rely heavily on written or electronically mediated communication, differing communication styles can cause misunderstandings. Ensure that you use unambiguous words and phrases, use visuals to explain complex ideas, and confirm understanding by seeking feedback wherever necessary.

Lack of non-verbal cues that clarify intent is a significant barrier in remote interactions. Try to include elements of informal conversation, use emojis where appropriate, or use video calls for more nuanced discussions to overcome this barrier. Despite the best efforts, at times, technical glitches pose significant communication hurdles. Prepare for these by ensuring a stable internet connection, using reliable software, and having a backup communication plan.

11.2. Leveraging Effective Communication Tools

In a digital world, a wide array of tools are available to aid in communication. Choosing the right one for the right purpose can often make a significant difference in understanding. Emails, chats and instant messaging, video conferencing, project management software, and social media each offer unique benefits and are better suited for certain types of communication.

Emails work well for formal communication and for documentation, but can lead to a delay in response. Instant messaging offers real-time interaction, but critical details might get lost in the flurry of messages. Video conferencing works best for complex discussions, brainstorming sessions, or for resolving conflicts. Project management tools are great for keeping everyone updated about project progress, while social media can facilitate lighter, more informal connections among team members.

11.3. Developing a Clear Communication Strategy

A well-articulated communication strategy, that takes into account the diversity of the teams, the complexity of the work, and the communication tools available, can significantly reduce miscommunication. It would outline the preferred mode of communication for various scenarios, expected response times, protocols for escalation, and how to document and share important details.

It's crucial to expect and respect diversity in the team's communication preferences and needs. Providing multiple modes of communication, providing flexibility in response times where possible, and offering resources and training can help in catering to these different requirements.

11.4. Building Trust Remotely

Trust building is undoubtedly more challenging in a remote scenario, but not impossible. Recognise that trust is built over time, through a series of consistent actions and interactions.

Transparency is a key factor. Make sure that roles, responsibilities, and expectations are clearly understood by everyone. Ensure everyone has access to the information they need to do their work effectively.

Consistency in communication, in policies, and in actions solidifies the trust. Recognize good work, provide constructive feedback, and treat every team member fairly to build and maintain trust.

Fostering a sense of team spirit is also crucial. Organize online team building activities, and find ways to create virtual 'water cooler moments'.

11.5. Navigating Difficult Conversations

Having difficult conversations remotely can be an intimidating task. However, designing your communication carefully, showing empathy, and recognizing the unique challenges posed by the remote environment can make this easier.

Choose the right time and the right platform for the conversation, use an empathetic and respectful tone, offer solutions, and seek feedback throughout the process. If necessary, involve a neutral third-party in the conversation.

11.6. Review and Improve

Finally, like any other strategy, your communication strategy must also be an evolving one. Constantly review and improve it based on feedback from team members, changes in team composition and needs, and advancements in communication tools and strategies.

To navigate through miscommunications and build trust in a digitally-mediated work environment requires understanding the limitations and the possibilities of these platforms, adapting your communication strategy to include a variety of communication methods, and always ensuring transparency and consistency in your interactions. With these steps, your remote communication can be as effective, and as personal, as face-to-face communication, if not more.

www.ingramcontent.com/pod-product-compliance
Lightning Source LLC
Chambersburg PA
CBHW071010260726
48661CB00007B/2872